ENOUGH PEACE AND QUIET FOR A FULL DAY

REST STOPS

for

TEACHERS

ENOUGH PEACE AND QUIET FOR A FULL DAY

REST STOPS *for* TEACHERS

WRITTEN AND COMPILED BY

SUSAN TITUS OSBORN

Nashville,
Tennessee

REST STOPS FOR TEACHERS
Copyright © 2003 by Susan Titus Osborn
All Rights Reserved

Broadman & Holman Publishers, Nashville, Tennessee
ISBN 0-8054-2670-1

Dewey Decimal Classification: 242
Subject Heading: Teachers/Educators/Devotional Literature

Caseside printed in the United States. Text printed and bound in Mexico.
1 2 3 4 06 05 04 03

Contents

Dedication

To
My cousin, Heidi Carter,
and my dear friend, Linda Powell

These special teachers will leave a legacy behind
in the many young minds they will influence
during their teaching careers.

Introduction

The vocation that is thought to have the most profound effect on children and teens is that of teaching. During grade school, junior high, and high school, students spend more time with their teachers than with their parents or any other adult role model.

This situation offers a wonderful opportunity for us—as teachers—to mold these young lives, nurture their hearts, and challenge their minds. We can also set godly examples for them to follow, directing their paths in a positive direction. In order for us to offer opportunities for these young individuals to establish their values, they need to be able to see a Christlike image in us. If we inspire lifelong dreams in our young charges, they will remember us their entire lives.

The children of today come to the classroom in all stages of emotional and spiritual disrepair. Many are from broken homes or are living in single-parent families. Even in two-parent households, both parents often work, and little time or energy is left in the evenings to meet the needs of the kids. Some are near the breaking point; others are at decisive crossroads. To nurture these young people and point out the best route for them to take, we teachers need to walk closely with the Lord.

Many times, children come from families where the parents aren't the best role models. Parents don't always set an example by reading in front of their children. They may be too busy or—far too often—they may be unable to read. English may not be spoken in the home. If the students can't find role models at home, then they turn to their teachers to have this role fulfilled.

When I was growing up, the worst things that students were reprimanded for were chewing gum in the hallways, skipping school, and smoking behind the building. But our schools and the issues students face today are very different than they were forty years ago. Many schools have metal detectors to keep out guns and knives. Drug pushers try to infiltrate the campuses from grade schools to colleges. And the killings on school campuses have become too numerous to count. Today more than ever, children of all ages need the stability of good teachers to mentor them along the way so they can cope with the violence in their world.

If your classroom is large, finding time to give individual attention to students can be difficult. Each teacher must establish his or her own level of tolerance in terms of noise, physical activity, and talking. When you set goals for work accomplished and guidelines for behavior, you may find your parameters challenged and perhaps overrun by students who are constantly questioning your authority.

You overcome these obstacles in teaching through love and friendship—a friendship that needs to be expressed in words and deeds. Only God's grace can provide what you need to love all of your students regardless of their attitudes and behaviors.

And as you work to establish a balance in your *own* life, you will find a need for "rest stops" along the way—little respites in which to replenish your inner strength to be able to cope in the classroom for another day. Your tranquility must not be determined by those around you, but rather by the guiding of the Holy Spirit within you.

The call of teaching is a high call from the Master Principal. We are called to train the minds of children in God's image. To achieve this the students must be able to see a Christlike image in us. May our prayer be that God will use us as His instruments to touch these young lives and accomplish His purposes.

Part One
SETTING AN EXAMPLE

Our actions often speak much louder than our words, especially when our audience is children. How we act in the classroom, how we set our standards, and how we respond to our students sets a tone that our young charges will model. And they are watching us carefully. Many of these students don't have positive role models at home, so whether they are aware of it or not, they are depending on us for their ethical and moral values. If we are teaching in secular schools, we may not be able to share our Christianity openly, but they will see Him in our lives by our Christlike actions.

Come, children, listen to me;
I will teach you the fear of the Lord.
—PSALM 34:11

College
AT AGE FORTY

The thought of returning to college at age forty was scary! Could I handle the workload of balancing school, home responsibilities, driving my sons to all their activities, and teaching a women's Bible study at church? I wasn't really sure. But I had started writing Christian articles and stories five years earlier. To gain a strong enough biblical foundation to do that as capably as possible, I felt like I needed more education. So I decided to take classes at our local university.

Once I returned to school, though, I knew I would have to carve out of an already busy schedule a large chunk of time for studying, writing papers, and taking tests. What I *didn't* know was whether or not I could learn to study again and retain what I needed to pass my courses.

I shared my dreams and fears with a dear friend at church who fortunately also happened to be the religious studies department chairman at our local university. "I'm toying with the idea of returning to school, Don. I had to drop out of college nineteen years ago when my father was killed in an accident. I've always wanted to obtain my degree, but the timing hasn't seemed right before."

"What do you want to major in, Susan?" he asked.

"Religious studies," I replied. "I've been asked to write my first book, *Parables for Young Teens*, and I'd like to get more theology under my belt if I'm going to write curriculum and Bible studies."

"I think your returning to college is a wonderful idea," Don said, excitement filling his voice. "I can help you plan your classes so that the ones you take will benefit your writing the most."

"That would be great," I replied, but then I paused. "I'm scared. Most of the other students will be half my age, and they are used to studying. I haven't studied in nineteen years!"

Don chuckled. "You will make a wonderful student, Susan; you are serious and focused. The younger students are more worried about what to wear, how their hair looks, and who they are going out with on Saturday night than they are with their studies. You have a supportive family and won't be distracted by nonsensical issues."

Don convinced me that I could handle the load, so I enrolled the following semester, signing up for three classes. I had to budget my time carefully, but I was able to balance my activities without neglecting my family or my studies.

I took a number of Don's classes, which were interactive and thought-provoking, not just an exercise in memorization. During the five years I worked on my undergraduate degree, Don always had an encouraging word for me when I saw him in the halls, at church, or in class. He said, "I know God has great things planned for you, Susan. He is going to use you in a magnificent way."

During those years, Don mentored me through my courses, through a heart-wrenching divorce, and through turning an avocation of writing into a full-time career. He encouraged me to go on to graduate school, and eventually I received an M.A. in communication. Many of the concepts Don taught me I continue to use in the books I write and the courses I teach today.

Ten years after I started back to college, Don performed the ceremony for my second marriage. Don died a few years later, but his teaching and encouraging words continue to live in my heart and my head. I am now a published author of twenty-five books as well as an adjunct professor, and I owe a great deal of thanks to this special mentor whose encouragement began during the writing of my first book. Don taught me to step out in faith and to trust the Lord to lead the way.

—*Susan Titus Osborn*

The things taught in school are not an education but a means to an education.

—RALPH WALDO EMERSON

ARE YOU THE SUB?

The regular teacher expected a different substitute. He saw me and looked worried. "I don't want to insult you, but this class needs somebody mean!"

My heart sank. The "mean routine" had never worked well for me. Normally I substituted in elementary school. But this, an experimental English class, was for problem high school students. I was afraid he was right. Panic surged, but I pushed it back.

"Good luck!" he said. "I have to leave now." With these words, the frowning teacher hurried out the door. Soon a herd of teens sauntered into the room, leaving me barely enough time to whisper, "Lord, I can't handle this without your help. Please give me the words to say."

Wearing insolence like uniforms, they looked me over. "Are you the sub?" a tattooed-and-nose-pierced boy asked incredulously.

I met his eyes and nodded. The bell rang. Several kids hitched themselves onto the wide windowsills. Others scraped chairs across the floor to sprawl in noisy groups.

Walking to the front of the room, I waited, not saying a word. Inexplicably, my panic ebbed away as one by one the kids turned to eye me. I heard myself speaking quietly: "Your teacher explained that you already have your assignment. I'm here to help you all I can. I will not make you work. That's up to you. I'll only ask that if you decide not to work, you won't disturb those who *are* working."

The kids sat in surprised silence. Then some pupils began to write. Others opened books. The rest resumed talking, but in softer voices.

I moved around the room, listening in on conversations that made me realize how sheltered my life had been.

"I'm so tired I can't even think," a girl whose blonde hair needed a good shampoo told another with many tiny braids. "Someone told my boyfriend that I talked to Pete. He started pounding on me. I got away, but I knew he'd be watching for me if I went home. I snuck into somebody's shed and hid there all night."

"You should have called the police," I offered.

"The police? You kidding?"

In a corner several boys talked about one of the students who wasn't in class. "Yeah, he got cut up pretty bad."

Cut up? How? In a gang fight? I didn't dare ask.

Other kids talked matter-of-factly about witchcraft involvement, ugly sexual entanglements, chaos at home, drugs.

This was normal, everyday life for these kids. No wonder their self-control was spread thin. Something (or Someone) held me back from giving orders or scolding when disruptions threatened. Instead, I moved to each situation with a question or a quiet comment that indicated I expected the best from the students involved. To my surprise this seemed to be enough to defuse the budding problem.

Perhaps the class didn't accomplish much academically that day. But I learned a valuable lesson: Brash though they appeared, these were hurting kids who needed my genuine concern and God's love.

I also learned another lesson. The God who cared enough to answer a frightened substitute's panicked whisper also showed her that she didn't have to be mean to accomplish the job.

—*Joan Rawlins Biggar*

A version of this piece was published in *Evangel* magazine, Feb. 21, 1988.

Remember not only to say the right thing in the right place, but far more difficult still, to leave unsaid the wrong thing at the tempting moment.

—BENJAMIN FRANKLIN

A Lesson in
FORGIVENESS

Annie had apparently been particularly bad that day. One complaint led to another as the other children reported instances of the insults and mistreatment she had inflicted.

I took Annie aside and whispered to her quietly. She vehemently denied any wrongdoing. When Eddie reported that he had been pinched by her (the redness of his arm testifying to the fact), I told Annie, "Stay in the room with me during noon recess."

Annie came in at noon, sat down, and finished her math. Eddie soon came in to finish his math, too. When they both brought their papers to me at about the same time, I checked their work quickly and then said to Annie, "Do you have something to say to Eddie?"

She looked at him. "I'm sorry. I don't know why I did that. I wish . . . I really wish I wouldn't do things like that."

"That's okay." Although Eddie's chin was quivering, the incident was over. His expression showed that he had completely forgiven her.

The other children came in from lunch recess, and we all settled down for story time. I noticed Annie didn't join us. Since she had offended so many other children, I supposed, she was just holding back. Yet I felt deep down that she wanted to be a part of the group.

I went over to her, pulled her close, and asked, "Do you have something you want to say to the other children?"

I breathed a sigh of relief as she walked to the front of the class. But when she stood in front of the group, she remained silent and looked hostile again.

Surprised by this unexpected flare-up of nerve, I spoke very authoritatively to Annie, "Please return to your seat. When you have something to say, you can rejoin the group." All the while I prayed I was doing the right thing.

After I read the last page of the story to the children, Annie came to me and whispered, "I have something to say now."

I stopped and told the children that Annie was going to speak.

The happiest people are less forgetting and more forgiving.

—AUTHOR UNKNOWN

Slowly, with difficulty, she began. "I'm so sorry I've been mean to you. I'm sorry I pulled your hair. I didn't mean to kick you. I'm sorry I spit on you. I really don't want to be that way!"

Spontaneously, the children cheered and clapped.

Annie smiled as she sat down and nestled in among the group. And even though the other children had not mistreated *her*, they began to say, "We're sorry, too! We didn't treat you as we should."

It happened just that simply. When Annie said she was sorry, it was over and done with. Case closed. Other infractions of the rules might occur in the future, but they would be dealt with as they happened. As far as this particular incident was concerned, it had ended there.

What a clear testimony this was to the simple relief of confession and the power of forgiveness. I resolved in my own life to practice the loving and forgiving spirit of a child. I would forgive those who had wronged me and resolve not to carry a grudge. Even though I didn't think the other children had offended Annie, they still said they were sorry. As an adult I needed to follow their example.

Forgiveness works at any age.

—*Joan Clayton*

Part Two
MOLDING LIVES

Children are so impressionable—from toddlers to teens. They are like clay in a potter's hand, pliable and easy to mold. Plus, they aren't afraid to show their emotions. When our students are having a problem at home or difficulty getting along with a bully in the classroom, that's our opportunity to show them compassion, concern, and empathy. When they are excited over a new goal or accomplishment and are bubbling over with enthusiasm, we can share in their laughter and joy.

Love is patient; love is kind. Love does not envy; is not boastful; is not conceited; does not act improperly; is not selfish; is not provoked; does not keep a record of wrongs; finds no joy in unrighteousness, but rejoices in the truth; bears all things, believes all things, hopes all things, endures all things.

Love never ends.

—1 CORINTHIANS 13:4-8

Behind
THE MASK

I had been forewarned about her. The college administration said she was unruly and hard to handle—a real troublemaker. I'll call her Shannon, although that was not her real name. But as I looked at this twenty-year-old girl, I wondered what lay behind her tough exterior. Would I be able to venture behind that mask?

Shannon was in the fiction writing class I taught at a local Christian college. I had told the students that although we would do a number of projects, they would work on one fiction story all semester. I suggested that they base their story on a true experience or something they were familiar with so they could really bring it to life. They would polish and fine-tune it over fifteen weeks and read it to the class on the final day. They would also be required to send it to a magazine as their final assignment.

The fourth week they all turned in first drafts of their stories. As I began to read Shannon's story, it seemed so real that chills ran down my spine. She told about a teen who was repeatedly beaten with a leather belt by her father. Her dad was a local pastor, well-respected in the church and community, while the girl was a rebel. No one believed her story.

I prayed for Shannon as I read her story a second time. Then I took a leap of faith and made myself vulnerable. At the bottom of her paper, I wrote, *If this is your true story, please stay after class. I would like to talk to you.*

The following Monday night, class ended at 9:00 p.m.

By 8:59 all the students had collected their personal belongings and were ready to bolt out of the door—all except Shannon. After everyone left she slowly collected her books and papers, staring at the floor the entire time. Then she shuffled up to my desk.

"Have a seat, Shannon," I said. "I'd like to talk to you for a few minutes."

She nodded her head, sat down, and finally made eye contact with me. No longer did I see a tough mask but the face of a vulnerable young lady who had been crushed by life.

"This is your personal story, isn't it, honey?" I asked softly.

"Yes, but no one believes me," she stammered.

"I believe you, Shannon," I said emphatically. "No one could write with the depth of emotion you did and not have experienced the circumstances."

She looked shocked. No one had believed her before. Her mother was in denial, shocked that Shannon would make up such stories. The church members thought her dad was a saint. *How could he mistreat his own child?* In the eyes of everyone who knew her, she was just a rebel, making up stories.

We talked for a long time. I told her that although I only taught on Monday nights, I was always in the office by late afternoon. "If you ever need to talk, I'm here for you, Shannon. Just stop by. And remember that soon you will graduate, and you'll start a life of your own—away from your parents, away from this community."

She nodded meekly, tears filling her eyes.

"God knows what happened," I continued, "and He will take care of you. He will also hold your parents accountable for what they have done. That's His job, not yours. Your job is to be everything God wants you to be."

She smiled through her tears and rose to go. Before leaving she held out her hand in an attempt to shake mine, but I put my arms around her and hugged her. Then I said, "If you aren't comfortable reading that story out loud in class, you can read one of your other assignments. I'll understand."

The last day of class, Shannon stood and proudly read her story. Of course the class didn't know it was really *her* story, and she did an excellent job. Plus, I saw a measure of healing take place through the sharing of her secret—with me, with the printed page, and with God.

—*Susan Titus Osborn*

Love does not consist of doing great things, rather love consists of doing small things with great love.

—MOTHER TERESA

Valuable
IN GOD'S EYES

As a child, Liz was a bookworm, reading everything from Dr. Seuss to Nancy Drew to Kurt Vonnegut. Her childhood scrapbooks were stuffed with illustrated stories, poetry, and short stories she had authored. By fifth grade she had finished writing her first full-length "book."

A year later Liz had grown to five-foot-six and was one of the tallest kids in her sixth-grade class. Her height, plus a desire to earn a coveted varsity letter, prompted her to try out for Lititz Elementary School's basketball team.

After surviving the first cut, Liz spent extra time practicing, dreaming of becoming a basketball star. She was great at jumping and learning the fundamentals, but she lacked speed and coordination.

One day her coach pulled her aside and said, "Child, you have so much talent—but not in basketball. I've read your stories, and they're good. *Really* good. I'm going to have to drop you at the next cut, but I wanted you to know why. You need to be writing, not dribbling a basketball."

At first Liz's heart seemed broken. After all, the school had no "writing team." But later that incident became her first clear memory of being encouraged to write. Liz reflected, "What a blessing to look back and see God's hand at work way back then, nudging me through this teacher's honest direction. It takes a special kind of courage to sit a child down and disappoint her, even while you're trying to steer her toward something better."

Liz took a leap of faith and showed one of her handwritten "mystery novels" to her sixth-grade teacher, Mrs. Smith. Instead of pointing out the mistakes, Mrs. Smith challenged her with positive suggestions for future books, urging her to keep writing. Liz wrote ten more books, mostly mysteries and love stories, before she turned seventeen. She hoped to become a published author.

Liz recalled that time: "Given anything to do with words—grammar, literature, drama, creative writing—I was in heaven!"

Sally Watkins, her eleventh-grade English teacher, honed Liz's skills and consistently praised her writing. "Something as simple as a three-word comment—'This is great!'—on my term paper meant the world to me," commented Liz.

By 1977 Liz transitioned to college radio, leading to a full-time career as a popular commercial radio personality. After marrying her husband, Bill, in 1986, she started speaking across the country and writing more. In 1990, with two children (ages one and three) and a very supportive husband, she graduated from Bellarmine College at age thirty-six.

When Liz signed a three-book contract with Thomas Nelson Publishers in 1992, she realized her basketball coach had done her a favor by redirecting her efforts to writing.

After authoring fourteen best-selling books, including her Gold Medallion winning *Parable* children's series, Liz returned home to Lititz, Pennsylvania, in April 2000 for the release of her second novel, *Bookends*, which is set in Lititz. Spotting Sally Watkins at her book signing, Liz waved toward her wide array of books and said, "Mrs. Watkins, this is all your fault!"

Liz noted, "What a blessing it was to see my teacher and to let her know, finally, what a difference her encouragement made in my choice of careers."

Being an "encourager" has become Liz Curtis Higgs's trademark and ministry. Her books encourage women to believe that they are beautiful, loved, and valuable "as is" in God's eyes.

—*LeAnn Weiss*

This story originally appeared in *Hugs for Teachers*, by LeAnn Weiss, copyright 2001. Reprinted by permission of Howard Publishing Company.

At the beginning, I was only a little mass of possibilities. It was my teacher who unfolded and developed them.

—HELEN KELLER

In the Grip of a Dumb, Old
DROOPY PERSPECTIVE

Children are likely to live up to what you believe of them. —LADY BIRD JOHNSON

Our son had managed to float unnoticed through third grade, and we were hoping for a bit more involvement from his fourth-grade teacher. John Mark's three older sisters were excellent students, but we didn't really know what to expect academically from our adopted son.

The boy was two-and-a-half when I first met him. It was his first time ever out of his broken crib and that dark room full of quiet children. Despite being scrawny and unused to walking on anything but a lumpy mattress, he still managed to push his way through a crowd of heftier Gypsy children in order to climb up into my arms.

I didn't want to be the one who chose the child we were meant to adopt. I prayed the night before that God would set something in the right child's heart for us, not just in *our* hearts for *him*. And God answered my prayer.

John Mark was an anxious little boy from the start, eager to please and surprisingly remorseful when he did the slightest thing wrong. We adored him, but he had a hard time letting love sink in. If he made a mistake in his schoolwork, he would call himself cruel names. We had to hug him from behind his back at times like these, because he couldn't look us in the eye.

On the first day of fourth grade, the students were told to share something about themselves with their new teacher. John Mark's eyes were forever fixed on the ground. He could only think of two things different enough about himself to be of any interest.

"I was born in Romania," he said when it was his turn, slightly proud of his exotic heritage. Then, in full Eeyore mode, he apologized, "And I'm a C student." A funeral dirge filled his voice. It was the mournful sound of someone who had given up on ever being good enough.

A lesser teacher might have thought the most loving way to handle such a statement was sympathy. A flimsier woman might have been embarrassed and speechless. But not Miss Gehl. She let him have it.

"Young man, look at me!" she ordered.

John Mark preferred to blend into the wallpaper, but being obedient was part of his nature. He looked up, just in case she was actually speaking to him.

"You are *not* a C student. You are *becoming* an A student. Do you hear me?"

Was this woman talking to him? He finally nodded like an awkward marionette whose head was being jerked up and down. Then when he thought he was safe, he returned to the familiar slouch of the depressed.

"Repeat this after me, John Mark," the surprising woman commanded. " 'I am on my way to becoming an A student.' "

Surely not.

When Miss Gehl made it clear she was serious, John Mark muttered the words under his breath.

"Say it again, this time *as if you mean it!*"

This teacher was tough. It must have been ten times she made him say those very same words.

"Louder, John Mark. Say it with conviction, '*I* am becoming an *A* student!' "

It went on like that until John Mark actually laughed, affirming this ridiculously hopeful statement about himself with such volume that the principal across the hall peeked into the room.

By the end of the school year, John Mark did end up making mostly A's. His countenance and posture changed remarkably. And all this happened thanks to a teacher stubborn enough to fight for the boy trapped inside a deadly perspective, a teacher who refused to allow a boy's eyes to grovel when God had made them to shine.

—*Cia Chester McKoy*

Part Three
DIRECTING PATHS

No matter what age we are dealing with in our classrooms, we are in a position where the effect we have on these young lives can be tremendous. The early impressions a child receives from our teaching may influence his or her life for years to come. Often we hear a person say something like, "I chose this vocation because of the encouragement I received from my seventh-grade math teacher." Or "I will never forget my high school English teacher and what he taught me." In order to be effective in directing the paths of our students, we need to pray and study God's Word so we can allow God to direct our paths.

I will speak mysteries from the past—
things we have heard and known and
that our fathers have passed down to us.
We must not hide them from their
children, but must tell a
future generation the
praises of the Lord.
—PSALM 78:2-4

31

A Student
NAMED BRAD

The first day of class, he immediately caught my eye. He sat in the front row and smiled at me while he furiously scribbled notes as I gave my lecture. I was teaching "Writing for the Workplace" at a local Christian university.

After class he waited until the other students left before walking up to my desk. "I'm a foreign student from Korea, and I just arrived in the U.S. last week. I'd prefer you called me Brad, rather than by my Korean name," he said.

"Okay, then . . . Brad," I agreed. "I'll mark that on the sheet." But we both knew this wasn't his main reason for stopping by my desk.

He continued, "I'd really like to take this class. I know I would benefit from it, but I think it's going to be too hard for me."

As I stared at this tall, serious young man, a still, small Voice inside me whispered, *Encourage him to stay in your class. You know he can handle the work.*

I paused for a moment, forming my words. Then I said, "I really think you can handle this class. I'll help you. I've taught short-term writing seminars in India, Taiwan, Nigeria, and the Philippines. I've worked with a lot of foreign students."

Brad's face lit up. "Oh, you've taught other people who had English as a second language?" he replied.

"Yes. Almost all my students in those countries had English as a second language." Wanting to be sure I gave him all the encouragement I could, I asked, "Do you eat dinner on campus, Brad?"

"Yes, usually."

"Well, whenever you have questions about your lessons, then, you could sit with me at dinner and ask."

"Oh, thank you, Professor Osborn. I would feel honored to eat dinner with you."

"Wonderful. I'll meet you outside the cafeteria at five o'clock next Tuesday," I said.

As it turned out, I ate with Brad almost every Tuesday night. I went to those dinners expecting to help him with his studies, but I was in for a surprise. He actually needed no guidance for the class whatsoever.

Instead, I was the one who did most of the learning. He introduced me to other Asian students, who were fascinating to talk with. He gave me insight on America from a foreign student's viewpoint. He told me the problems he faced by not having a car, which made it hard for him to shop and go places with the limited amount of mass transit available in Southern California. "I'd like to attend a Korean church and eat Korean food. American food is so bland," he said. "And most of all I miss my girlfriend."

He also gave me tips on how to improve my teaching methods. He suggested I shorten the lecture times and make the sessions more interactive. The student became the teacher, and the teacher became the student.

When the final grades were in, Brad received the highest grade in the class. He commented that he had learned a great deal from me. Yet he didn't realize how much I had learned from him.

During his first semester in America, Brad developed confidence in his abilities to achieve in a different culture. Someday he will return to Korea armed with an excellent education, and I'm convinced he will be an asset to his home country as a business leader.

Sometimes all we have to do is encourage them, and who knows where they'll end up?

—*Susan Titus Osborn*

True teaching, then, is not that which gives knowledge, but that which stimulates pupils to gain it.

—MILTON GREGORY

The Class
BODYGUARD

Jimmy was big for his age. He towered above my other second-grade students and outweighed them by at least twenty pounds. Being so robust and strong made him the number one choice for soccer at recess, but the game always ended with complaints and skinned knees.

"Jimmy knocked me down!"

"Jimmy made me bump my head."

"Jimmy tore my shirt."

"Jimmy kicked the ball in my face."

I tried several methods. Making Jimmy the referee was not a good choice. That solution put Jimmy in the thick of the game. I changed "free play" into directed activities, only to hear, "When are we going to get to play soccer?" I banned soccer playing for awhile, only to hear the same complaints about Jimmy's roughness on the playground.

Jimmy was not an aggressive child. He loved to play, and he really didn't mean to hurt other children. It just kind of happened because of his size and awkwardness. I prayed for guidance. I needed wisdom in providing the best I could for each child in the class.

One day Jimmy complained to me, "Nobody likes me. Nobody plays with me. I don't have any friends." Tears streamed down his face.

I could feel his hurt, and I prayed for the right words before saying, "Jimmy, you are a very special boy. You are big and strong, and that's good. But you see, the other children are much smaller, and they are not big and strong like you. I know you don't mean to run into anyone or accidentally bump someone.

"But I'll tell you what: Since you are so strong, why don't I make you the 'class bodyguard'? You can watch over the other children. You can be my assistant. When you see kids playing too rough or getting into trouble, you can remind them of our playground rules. Then you can show them how to play safely."

Jimmy loved the idea. He could hardly wait for the next recess. Neither could I!

I was overcome with gratitude for an answered prayer as I watched Jimmy mingle among the children. He walked around with a big smile on his face—protecting, helping, and defending. I was thrilled to see the children's reactions. They became extremely receptive and were visibly touched that Jimmy was cheering them on.

As the end of school approached, instead of hearing the children complain about their run-ins with Jimmy, I saw them hoping they would be in his room again in third grade. On the last day of school, I announced to them who their teachers would be for next year. There were many "hoorays" for those who were going to be in Jimmy's new room, and many disappointments for those who were not.

Jimmy told me good-bye, hugged me tightly, and ran to the bus. I went back to my classroom and cried.

After the third grade, Jimmy changed schools, and I lost track of him. But three years later during the summer, I received a surprise phone call from Jimmy.

"Hi, Mrs. Clayton! This is Jimmy. Remember me? I just wanted to call and tell you good-bye. We're moving to Kentucky. I'll never forget you, Mrs. Clayton. I'm even bigger and stronger! Thank you for teaching me that I can be big and strong, but still be soft and gentle."

—*Joan Clayton*

The way from God to a human heart is through a human heart.

—SAMUEL DICKEY GORDON

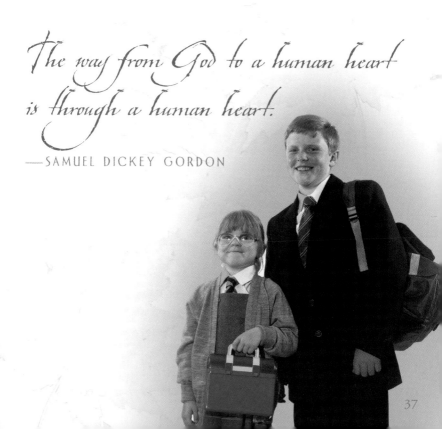

The Greatest
OF THESE

Let God love you through others,
and let God love others through you

—D.M. STREET

My day began on a sour note when I saw my six-year-old son wrestling with a limb of my azalea bush. By the time I got outside, he'd broken it.

"Can I take this to school today?" he asked.

With a wave of my hand, I sent him on his way. I turned my back so he wouldn't see the tears. I touched another limb of my favorite bush as if to say, *I'm sorry.*

I wished I had said those words to my husband earlier, but I'd been angry. The washing machine had leaked on my linoleum floor the night before. *If he'd just taken the time to fix it!* I was still mopping when Jonathan walked into the kitchen and asked, "What's for breakfast, Mom?"

I opened the nearly empty refrigerator. "How about toast and jelly?" I smeared the toast with jelly and set it

38

in front of him. *Why was I so angry?* I thought as I tossed my husband's dishes into the sudsy water. Later I managed to lug the wet clothes to the laundromat, thinking how love had disappeared from my life. Staring at wall graffiti, I felt as wrung out as the clothes in the washer.

I finished hanging up my husband's shirts and glanced at the wall clock. I was late. Jonathan's class was already out, so I dumped the clothes in the car and drove to the school. Knocking on the classroom door, I saw the teacher motion for me to wait. She said something to Jonathan and then handed him crayons and paper.

What now? I thought, as she rustled through the door.

"I want to talk to you about Jonathan," she said quietly.

I prepared myself for the worst. My husband and I already weren't speaking after the fight we'd had. My son had broken a limb off my favorite bush, and now this.

She continued, "Did you know Jonathan brought flowers to school today?"

I nodded, trying to keep the hurt in my eyes from showing. I glanced at my son busily coloring a picture. His long, wavy hair flopped just beneath his brow. He brushed it away, and I noticed his blue eyes shone as he admired his handiwork.

"See that little girl?" the teacher asked.

"Yes." I peered through the glass in the direction the teacher was pointing and saw an exuberant child laugh and point to a picture on the wall.

"Yesterday she was hysterical. Her mother and father are

going through a nasty divorce. She told me she didn't want to live—she wished she could die. I watched her bury her face in her hands and say loud enough for the whole class to hear, 'Nobody loves me.' I did all I could to console her, but it only seemed to make matters worse."

"I thought you wanted to talk to me about Jonathan," I said.

"I do," she said, touching my arm. "Today your son walked over to that little girl. I watched him hand her some pretty pink flowers and whisper, 'I love you.' "

I felt my heart swell with pride at what my son had done. Excusing myself, I smiled at the teacher as I opened the door, walked over to Jonathan's desk, and squeezed his hand. "You've made my day!" I whispered to him.

Later that evening, I pulled weeds from around my lopsided azalea bush. My mind wandered back to the love Jonathan showed the little girl. A Bible verse came to me: "Now these three remain: faith, hope and love. But the greatest of these is love." My son had put love into practice. And all day I had only thought of how angry I was with him and my husband.

I heard the familiar squeak of my husband's truck brakes as he pulled into the driveway. I snapped a small limb bristling with hot pink azaleas off my prized bush. As I did so, I felt the seed of love that God planted in my family beginning to bloom once again in me.

My husband's eyes widened in surprise when I handed him the flowers.

"I love you," I said.

—*Nanette Thorsen-Snipes*

Part Four
ESTABLISHING VALUES

Most children are vastly influenced by their peers. They seek acceptance by mimicking their fellow students or by doing what the ones they consider leaders ask or tell them to do. Sometimes this is good, but more often the peers do not exemplify the values a student should be establishing. Children want to know they are accepted and are considered valuable. That is why they are willing to do almost anything to belong to their peer group. As teachers we can affirm these needs while establishing high values in our students.

Teach a youth about the way he should go; even when he is old he will not depart from it.

—PROVERBS 22:6

It's Going to Be
A GREAT YEAR!

Following tradition the night before a new school year began, Marty, my husband, and I took each of our children aside and prayed with them, committing their school year to God. Soon it was Jason's turn. "Lord," my husband prayed, "I ask that You would bless Jason and his eighth-grade year. Help him to learn all You have for him, and may You provide for each of his needs. Amen."

That's it? I thought as my husband finished his prayer. *Jason's entering the eighth grade in a public school! Shouldn't you pray that he makes good friends, has great teachers, and stays on the straight and narrow?*

"Son, it's going to be a great year!" Marty concluded as Jason left the room.

The first week of school went by. Jason seemed to be happy with his schedule, teachers, and classes. Yet he also had a request. "Mom, Mr. Reid has asked me to become his teacher's assistant for his sixth period class. I really want to, Mom. Can I?"

"What class do you have sixth period now?"

"I have Spanish. But I can take Spanish my freshman year of high school. Won't you sign this permission slip?"

I took the permission slip and set it on the counter. Jason knew that I wanted to run this grand idea past his father. As I prepared dinner, I thought about Mr. Reid and what kind of man he was. "He's cool and understands kids!" I could hear Jason saying. Even though Mr. Reid was one of the youngest teachers at the school, he had gained the admiration of all the students, staff, and parents. I also knew that Mr. Reid's extra-curricular activities outside of school consisted of working with a youth group at a local church. In a conversation with him the previous year, Jason had told him that we were believers, too.

That night Marty and I sat down to discuss the possibility of Jason becoming a teacher's assistant. We ran through the list of jobs Jason told us he would have to perform. All of them seemed to be comprised of busywork, and we were certain that it would help Mr. Reid. Yet our decision to allow Jason to become Mr. Reid's teacher's assistant was not based solely on how Jason could help Mr. Reid but on what Jason could receive from him. We were only willing to allow our son to delay his

Spanish class in order for Mr. Reid to be a mentor to him.

Jason's eighth-grade year was truly a year to remember. He definitely grew in wisdom and stature. He had a godly man at a public school take the time to imprint his life upon him. I don't think any other teacher has had a greater influence on our son than Mr. Reid has.

Looking back, I remember Marty's prayer at the beginning of the school year. "Lord, I ask that You would bless Jason and his eighth-grade year. Help him to learn all You have for him, and may You provide for each of his needs." God did bless our son in ways we never expected—thanks to Mr. Reid.

—*Janet Lynn Mitchell*

Nothing is so potent as the silent influence of a good example.

—JAMES KENT

A Little
AT A TIME

Tall, slim, blonde, and beautiful, our fifth-grade teacher stood in front of the classroom. She said, "I promised to show you something extraordinary during our share time."

She held up a thick phone directory. Then she proceeded to rip it in half. A hush fell over our classroom until Tim called out, "How'd you do that?"

"Pretty amazing, huh?" Mrs. Castle said with a smile. "How do you think I did it?"

Sara raised her hand and said, "You must have strong muscles."

Mrs. Castle flexed her thin arm. There wasn't much show of muscle.

Another boy jumped up and shouted, "Magic!"

Mrs. Castle went over to the blackboard and wrote our ideas down. They were getting pretty silly. Doug stood up and showed a picture he'd drawn—a woman with a cape and the caption, *Mrs. Superman*. We all laughed, including Mrs. Castle.

"Do you want to know the right answer?"

"Yes!" We all chimed in.

"Watch carefully." Mrs. Castle held up another directory and tore it slowly. This time we could see that she tore the book a few pages at a time. "Just a few at a time. That's the secret."

Wow! Did she ever have our attention! And from that morning on, she would use the same concept no matter what she was teaching. With math she would say, "Learning our multiplication tables is easy, if we learn one at a time. Once we learn them they never change." At reading hour she would say, "Start

45

at the beginning of a book. Advance one page at a time, and by the end you'll know the story."

Soon I began to follow her advice at home: a little at a time when cleaning my room or helping with chores.

At Christmas she had a party at her house and played her harp for us. The next day she talked about how, after electing the harp as the instrument she wanted to play, she had first learned to read music before taking lessons.

My grandmother had tried to teach me to play the piano, but I never would cooperate. The next time I visited, I surprised her by showing interest. I even sat still long enough for her to teach me the keyboard. With each subsequent visit I'd practice musical exercises. Before long I could play "Mary Had a Little Lamb."

Unfortunately, I still struggled academically. Toward the end of the year, Mrs. Castle called me over to her desk and said, "Karen, I know that you have tried hard all year, but you need some extra help. That is why I'm holding you back a year."

Tears formed in my eyes. I thought, *Why did this have to happen?*

In youth we learn;
in age we understand.

—MARIE EBNER-ESCHERBACH

"Karen, there's a purpose for everything, even when it hurts. But someday you'll understand that hurts can make us strong. Just remember that to accomplish a lot, we have to start out just a little at a time."

In my youth I didn't appreciate what a wise woman my fifth-grade teacher was. But as an adult I understand that the concepts she taught me have helped me establish my values in many of life's governing factors—both the ones I had dominion over and circumstances beyond my control.

Mrs. Castle's instruction of "a little at a time" has turned out to be a powerful gift to me. When applied correctly, it is an exercise in wisdom that benefits our hearts. It creates a desire to learn and a determination not to give up.

—*Karen Kosman*

The Matchless
GIFT

After my second graders completed reciting the Pledge of Allegiance, they settled back into their seats. But Duane remained standing. Duane was an exceptionally bright and lovable student. His home life, however, was far from perfect.

His mother was a single parent who had many problems, including drinking and an abusive boyfriend. I feared for his safety because Duane was often burned with cigarettes while trying to protect his sisters. I had reported this to Social Services before, and Duane and his three younger sisters had been taken out of the home. But Social Services deemed it safe and kept returning them to their mother.

Thinking that maybe he'd had a bad night, I walked over to him to see what the matter was. As he looked up at me with those dark brown eyes, I could see his hurt and disappointment.

"Mrs. Brown, aren't you going to open my Christmas present?" he asked. "I put it on your desk."

As I glanced at my desk, all I could see was an avalanche of papers, stickers, and books. Seeing my puzzled look, Duane went to the front of the room and retrieved his gift from my desk. As he handed it to me, I noticed the wrapping paper was a napkin from the lunchroom.

Carefully removing the napkin, my gift appeared to be a matchbox. Although I had only been a teacher for three months, I had learned the important lesson of asking a child to explain a picture or (in this case) a gift rather than disappointing him with a wrong guess. So I said to Duane, "Tell me about your gift."

You give but little when you give of your possessions. It is when you give of yourself that you truly give.

—KAHLIL GIBRAN

"First of all," Duane instructed, taking the box in his hand, "you have to use your imagination before opening my gift. This isn't really a matchbox. It's a jewelry box." He held it up for me to see. Then he continued, "You'll find two precious gems inside." With that he handed me back my gift.

As I opened my jewelry box, I was surprised by the sight (as well as the smell) of two beer caps. "Those aren't beer caps," Duane informed me. "They're really two precious silver earrings. I've never seen you wear earrings, and I wanted you to have some pretty ones."

My eyes began to tear at the thoughtfulness of this child's precious gift. Since birth, one of my ears was slightly deformed. Fearing that wearing earrings might draw attention to the ear, I never wore them. But how could I not wear these precious earrings given by this special child? As I placed the earrings on my ears with masking tape, my class clapped, and Duane stood proudly beside me.

Every year after that, the matchbox remained on my desk. It reminded me of this child's kindness and the wonderful lessons he taught me. Duane gave all he had—his heart.

Although his situation at home was not the best, Duane continued to see the good in life. The beer caps were an ugly reminder of problems at home, but Duane had made them into something beautiful—two precious gems. Although my ear was deformed, Duane still wanted me to have pretty earrings. Even though the matchbox had held the matches that had lit the cigarettes that had painfully burned his skin, his surprisingly tender heart allowed us all to see it as a treasure box instead of a dangerous weapon.

Whenever I see Duane's gift on my desk, it encourages me. If I am having trouble reaching a student, I try to be like Duane and give that student a piece of my heart. When I am having a trying day, one glance at the matchbox reminds me of the small boy who had a trying day every day—as well as every night.

Out of the heart of a second-grade boy, one teacher will always have a gift to treasure.

—*Stephanie Ray Brown*

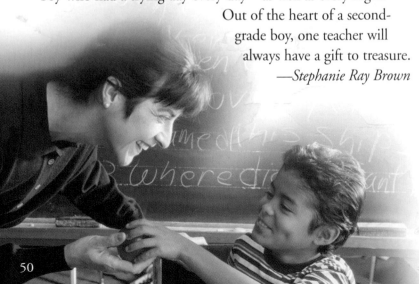

Part Five
AFFIRMING ACTIONS

Most children at one time or another will act up in class. The more control we have over the class and the more they have gained our respect, the less of a problem we are likely to have with this issue. As we encourage and affirm their positive actions while not tolerating the negative ones in the classroom, we are preparing them for the future. Our young charges need to realize that when we say no, we mean it. And when we give them a directive, they must respond—or there will be consequences.

Then the children were brought to Him so He might put His hands on them and pray. But the disciples rebuked them. Then Jesus said, Leave the children alone, and don't try to keep them from coming to Me, because the kingdom of heaven is made up of people like this.

—MATTHEW 19:13–14

Thank You,
MR. CLARK

A teacher affects eternity; he can never tell where his influence stops.

—HENRY ADAMS

"Hi, Susan! Guess who this is?" asked the man on the other end of the telephone.

I paused for a moment, trying to place his voice. It didn't sound familiar. "I'm sorry, but I don't recognize you," I answered hesitantly.

The man laughed. "Well, it's no wonder. After all, it's been twenty-two years."

My mind mentally did the math. It was 1984 now, so twenty-two years ago would have been 1962, the year I graduated from high school. I was still drawing a total blank, but I decided to take a wild stab. "Did I go to high school with you?" I asked hopefully.

He laughed again. "Close. This is Charles Clark, your high school English teacher. I was sorry that I missed your twentieth reunion. Your class was very special to me."

"Oh, Mr. Clark, it's great to hear from you. At the reunion I told people that the one teacher I wanted to talk to was you."

"Well, now's your chance," he replied. "I'm not teaching any-more, and I travel quite a bit for my job. I picked up one of the reunion booklets that you and Raye put together, so I've been calling students when I find myself in their hometowns. Now I'm in Southern California, so I called you. The booklet looks great. I see you've put to use the grammar, punctuation, and word usage I taught you."

"More than you could ever guess!" I exclaimed. "I've become a freelance writer. I've been writing articles and church school take-home papers. I went to my first writers' conference this year and just signed my first book contract with Standard Publishing House."

"That's great, Susan! I knew you had talent, but more than that, I knew you had perseverance and were willing to work hard."

I replied, "You always did encourage me to push a little harder, to polish my writing a little more. And more than that, you gave me a firm foundation. You taught me the basics so that the mechanics now come easily. That way, I can concentrate on the creative part."

We talked a little longer, and then Mr. Clark said, "I'd better go. I have a meeting with a customer, but I wanted to call you first."

"I'm so glad you did. Now I can say 'thank you' for telling me I could be all that God wanted me to be. Thank you, Mr. Clark."

That conversation took place eighteen years ago, but it seems like yesterday. My fortieth high school reunion is fast approaching, and somehow I hope Mr. Clark will be there. I want to tell him that I have now published twenty-five books, and that one of them was on the best-seller list. I've taught creative writing courses on four Christian college campuses and have used many of the teaching ideas I learned from Mr. Clark. I've also taught writing seminars in five countries and tried to make the concepts easy to understand, concrete, and as interesting as Mr. Clark did.

I'm thankful to God for bringing a wonderful English teacher into my life to set a wonderful example for me and to affirm my love for writing. And once again I'd like to say, "Thank you, Mr. Clark."

—*Susan Titus Osborn*

THE TIME

Jeff, a mediocre student, had not had a stellar year with me in the previous term, but we'd made out all right. Now I faced a new problem as I looked at my class list for the coming year. It included Jerry, Jeff's younger brother. I had already developed a history with him, and it was not a positive one. He was down-right irritating!

Jerry would often come by the classroom to see his brother. I constantly had to reprimand him for disrupting the class from the hallway and for being where he was not supposed to be. Our class had also put on a school play with Jerry's class the previous year, and I had endured Jerry's constant commentary throughout all the practices. He seemed uncomfortable with any silence.

One good thing, though: the prospect of having him at my elbow for an entire year certainly strengthened my prayer life. For the two weeks until school started, I prayed earnestly that I would be able to handle Jerry in a Christlike way that would still leave me sane.

Finally a plan materialized. I had learned early in my relation-ship with Jerry that speaking to him only brought a longer response in return. I had read that smiling uses fewer muscles and is much more relaxing than frowning. So I decided that whenever Jerry irritated me, I would simply smile at him.

Within the first twenty minutes of class on the first day, I tried out my plan.

As I was explaining how our day would go, the other twenty-four students watched me wide-eyed with their mouths closed and hands folded. Jerry, on the other hand, was strolling around the room. I stopped speaking and smiled at him.

Everyone else turned to look at Jerry, too, waiting for the usual teacher reprimand. But I just looked at him and smiled.

"I have to sharpen my pencil," he explained. Then, looking down at both of his empty hands, he said with his cheerful grin, "I guess I forgot and left it at my desk!"

I went back to my monologue. But once Jerry actually started paying attention, he was full of questions.

"Do we have recess in fifth grade?"

The task of the excellent teacher is to stimulate apparently ordinary people to unusual effort. The tough problem is not in identifying winners: it is in making winners out of ordinary people.

—K. PATRICIA CROSS

"How long do we get to stay outside after lunch?"

"Do we have to do the Revolutionary War project that my brother's class had to do last year?"

"Will we have a program that parents come to?"

"When do we get to meet the new gym teacher?"

His hand shot up every two minutes. Each time I smiled, answered briefly, and continued with the subject at hand.

His finest quality was consistency. He never quit asking questions and was always right in the middle of everything. It seemed that I could never escape his presence.

In the third week of school, I ran into his mother in the supermarket. Mrs. Parker approached me eagerly, smiling broadly. "Mrs. Boyd!" she exclaimed. "I am so glad to talk to you. I've been meaning to call you to tell you what a great year Jerry is having. He just loves his class, and he really loves you."

I was a little overwhelmed at such lavish praise from an ordinarily shy and defensive parent. I muttered something appreciative.

"Oh, yes!" she continued. "I ask him all the time how school is going, and he says it's going great." Her voice dropped a little. "And I'm so glad. You know Jerry has had some problems in the past with getting along with teachers. But he said, 'You know, Mom, I can tell Mrs. Boyd really likes me. She smiles at me all the time!'"

—*Lanita Bradley Boyd*

How Do You Spell
CAPITAL F?

Teachers open the door.
You enter yourself.

—CHINESE PROVERB

Beau was unforgettable—large, uncouth, nearly illiterate, but just happy to be in school. The desire of my teacher's heart was for Beau to read.

It seemed to me that his previous teachers had instilled in him all the necessary decoding skills.

And although I had no academic expertise in teaching reading, I felt that Beau just needed the opportunity to practice those skills. He had been mainstreamed from a special education class where the teacher read to him but had given him no chance to read for himself.

Beau deserved literacy, and I was determined that he achieve it.

I was blessed to have him in both my remedial English class and my study hall. The study hall met in the library, where the students sat around tables in an atmosphere more informal than that of a regular classroom. I shared Beau's table. Giving him *Thunderhead*, I said, "Beau, every day during this hour, you and I are going to read. While you silently read *Thunderhead*, I am going to sit across from you and silently read a book of my choice."

Beau accepted the assignment. Because he liked school, he was always willing to try. He read, I read, and I watched Beau read. On a good day he could read a page in about ten or fifteen minutes. Most days were not that good.

School had started in August. The temperature was nearly one hundred degrees every afternoon. The building had no air conditioning. So as Beau read, laboriously mouthing every word, pausing often to ask me for a pronunciation or a definition, sweat dampened his face and his shirt. He smudged the pages and the tabletop. I had no idea that reading could be such hard work. My sympathies grew as Beau struggled and sweated.

After eight days, Beau was on page eighteen, and I could no longer watch the struggle. I decided that I was going to read that book to him. No one should have to struggle that hard.

But Beau saved me. As if he sensed my uneasiness, he looked up from *Thunderhead*, smiled, and announced, "This here is the best book I ever read."

The entire school became involved in Beau's reading. He worked at it for at least forty minutes a day, requiring the entire first quarter to finish reading *Thunderhead*. But, my, how we all celebrated when he finished!

He had started *Where the Red Fern Grows* when a snowstorm stranded him at a relative's home for several days after Thanksgiving vacation. When he returned, Beau proudly announced, "I finished reading that dog book. I 'bout cried when they died."

And *I* 'bout cried to learn that he had taken a book with him on vacation. To think that he had read it was overwhelming.

Now Beau needed another book. Because he had enjoyed *Red Fern* so much, I suggested that he read *Old Yeller*. "I'm sure the middle school has a copy of it," I said to him. "I'll call them. We can have it here in the morning."

"If I kin read that book, I'm sure them little kids kin read it. It's probably in the grade school library across the street. I'll go get it."

The elementary library was a veritable candy store of literature for Beau. He unabashedly read book after book: *Old Yeller,* the *Black Stallion* series, and the ultimate—*Smoky, the Cow Horse*.

The other students stayed supportive:

"Hey, Beau, what are you reading?"

"How many books have you read, Beau?"

As Beau learned to read, he learned to write as well. At first he wrote seemingly disconnected ideas, then rudimentary sentences. Slowly he produced page after page, writing about the pain when his parents divorced, writing about the pet cow he and the other children used to saddle and ride, writing about school and how much he loved football.

When the time came for final editing, I returned their papers. When Beau received his, he pushed up his sleeves, wiped the sweat from his brow, and set to work. When I walked by him, he crushed my wrist in his sticky grip and demanded, "Hey, teacher, how do you spell capital F?"

I can assure you, "F" certainly wasn't his final grade.

—*Lonnie C. Crowe*

Part Six
OFFERING OPPORTUNITIES

Next to a child's parents, we teachers probably have more effect on a child's development than anyone else in their lives. This sphere of influence can include social, academic, and even spiritual things. That is why our care and concern needs to stretch beyond the subjects we teach. We need to get to know our students personally. By establishing a friendship with our students and being willing to listen to what they have to tell us, we will be remembered by them much longer than the duration of a school year.

I am able to do all things through Him who strengthens me.

—PHILIPPIANS 4:13

Gold Stars
FOR A WRITER

As our second-grade class watched in wonder, Miss Stevens cleared a large space on her bulletin board. She covered it with glorious blue paper surrounded by large gold stars. Across the top she placed a banner: "Our Very Best Writing."

"Children," she explained, "now that you are learning cursive, this is where I will put up our class's very best handwriting work. So I want all of you to try extra hard. See how many of you can have papers up there for Parents' Night!"

My heart sank. For weeks I had been dutifully trying to make D's and L's and all the rest on wide-lined yellow paper. My father had learned elegant Spenserian script before he was five. My mother, a former schoolteacher, wrote as gracefully as a work of art. As for me, my letters seemed to tumble all over each other as if they'd been dumped out of a can of nails!

Each day we did our assignments. And each day four or five were selected for that great place of honor. The day before Parents' Night, I was the only student not represented.

"Don't worry, Bonnie," my teacher said. "Your arithmetic papers are up. And so are your spelling papers." But that wasn't the same. I wanted to be a writer. How could I be a writer if I couldn't write?

During the Depression, most of us children couldn't afford tablets to write on. So each day we were given sheets of paper to do our homework on that night. The last evening before Parents' Night, I filled up one sheet with math problems, one with spelling words, and one with a tumble of excruciatingly difficult cursive letters. How unsatisfying it all was! I wanted to write! But now I had no paper left to write on.

Then I found a sheet of scrap blue paper my father had brought home from work. One side was filled with words and numbers, but the back was completely bare. None of those horrible lines to have to stay in! So on it I printed a poem that I made up on the spot. And then another and another. I stuck them in corners. I wrote along the edges. I filled every single inch—not with great literature, but with rhymes I made up that expressed what was on my childish heart. Hoping against hope, I took the sheet to school the next day and showed it to Miss Stevens.

That evening when all the parents piled into our classroom, everyone was completely taken by the wonderful board full of "Our Very Best Writing." No, my work was not there. But in a special place—all by itself—was a sheet of red paper also bordered with gold stars. Over this one she had written, "Our Very Best *Writer*." And right in the middle was my page full of rhymes.

People to this day look at my handwriting and say, "Why, you must be a doctor!" Yes, it's that illegible. So I print—and sometimes *I* can't even read it! Back when I taught second grade myself, my students did better work than I did.

But how thankful I am that one teacher could look beyond my complete lack in that area and see with me my hopes and dreams. To look at a scribbled sheet of crumpled paper and call me a writer! To believe in me enough that I indeed became one!

—*Bonnie Compton Hanson*

Good teachers make the best
of a pupil's means:
great teachers foresee a pupil's ends.

—MARIA CALLAS

He Let Who
DO WHAT?

"What's your favorite subject in school?"

I was a little embarrassed by my answer. What would my father think? I loved earning candy in math, and the creative projects in English were cool, but *shop* had my heart. It was the only class I raced to and hated to leave. I fell in love with woodworking because of a towering, bald-headed carpenter who wore a heavy green apron and was prone to whisper, "Does that feel like the belly of a baby duck yet to you?"

Cal Cooper was the original tough and tender male, and I adored him. He taught us sixth graders how to sand our wood projects until our cheeks could enjoy their softness and how to carve out bowls using a lathe. This sixty-year-old man held our undivided attention with few words and piercing eyes. His class was serious business. The tools were not toys, and if we didn't listen to his instructions, we might lose a finger.

Given the risks inherent in his trade, it's all the more surprising that Cal gave in to two twelve-year-old girls' pleadings. He let my cousin and me break from the traditional "curriculum" and make a giant wooden disc that we intended to pull behind our grandparents' speedboat that summer—with us on it. Cal broke his cardinal rule about only letting high school kids use any power tool besides the lathe. He gave us access to the powerful band saw and electric sander.

In 1966 no magazine articles stressed the importance of empowering young women. Cal just did it, and because of it, Alice and I went beyond being two wide-eyed girls able to follow directions that year.

The world is a narrow place when you're twelve, and one's dreams are comparatively small. Ours was a goofy, unwieldy project, but that wasn't the point. Cal Cooper, our beloved "Gentle Giant," was willing to let us try to do what we longed to do, knowing we could possibly hurt ourselves in the process.

Did he intuitively know that a far greater hurt might come from squelching the enthusiastic initiative of young people, from forcing them into a small box they were built to escape?

Did some kind, older man trust *him* with dangerous tools prematurely and thereby help shape him into the grateful, confident man he is today?

I don't know why he said "yes" to us. His attention during our class time would be all the more divided, and his anxiety level would inevitably be raised. All this for two pesky girls.

Thirty-six years later, though, I'm still building odd things with power tools. I trace my confidence to one decision made by one man. My shop teacher's open-mindedness meant I would never swallow my dreams no matter how seemingly silly, the way so many compliant girls do.

Cal Cooper pushed us all further than we wanted to go, especially in sanding our finished work, but he also dared trust us to chart our own course. It's a legacy at least as appealing as the soft underbelly of a baby duck.

—*Cia Chester McKoy*

Sometimes learning is more caught than taught.

—AUTHOR UNKNOWN

The Web
TEAM

It was Dustin's junior year of high school when we told him we were moving from Utah to Tennessee. We realized that familiar friends and teachers would be numerous miles away, and the uncertainty of moving a student who was near graduation caused our family great concern!

In addition Dustin suffers with Crohns, an inflammatory bowel disease. Transitioning into a new school and making new friends would probably create more stress. Dustin's stomach pains conceivably could become more persistent. Yet through prayer we believed God would work out every detail.

Soon it was time for the family to make the long trip to Tennessee and for Dustin to say good-bye to his friends and teachers. We realized we would need to leave a few hours earlier than we intended because a winter storm was imminent. The predictions from the local weather stations estimated ten inches of snow was due within hours!

I rushed to school to pick up Dustin and told him, "We need to leave Utah before the storm reaches here, or driving will be dangerous." Dustin nodded and followed me out to the car. As he climbed in, many of his classmates who were standing around started to shed tears. I had to choke back my own emotions as I drove Dustin to the empty house that soon would be our past.

The first two hours on the road seemed extremely tense as we traveled in silence. It was evident Dustin loved his school, teachers, and friends. And the stress of leaving them behind began to cause his disease to flare up the more miles we drove and the more hours that passed. Two thousand and two miles later, we arrived in Tennessee.

Dustin had two weeks to unpack, set up his bedroom, and celebrate Christmas before it was time to return to school. When the first day arrived, Dustin enrolled in the classes required to complete his junior year.

It wasn't very long before Dustin's computer teacher noticed something exceptional about him. Mrs. Roe quickly declared, "Dustin is the most technically knowledgeable student in the class." After spending several days talking with him, she discovered just the right responsibility for him.

Dustin's goals are to go to college and study in the field of computer engineering. Consequently, Mrs. Roe introduced him to a couple of other students with similar interests. How quickly she discerned what would make him feel like a part of his new school!

Within a few weeks Dustin's computer teacher asked him if he'd like to help update the school website. A school web team had been formed, and Dustin became actively involved in new friendships formed there.

When the mind is given opportunity, the heart will triumph!

—MYRA J. MARTIN

"I'm so glad my teacher offered me this opportunity!" he said.

The last week of school, Dustin put the finishing touches on the school website! As a result Mrs. Roe gave him a S.W.A.T. award, which stands for Students with Advanced Technology. She had not only offered him opportunity but had showed a caring heart for her new student.

Transferring from one school to another in teen years can be difficult. But Dustin's teacher sincerely tuned in with her newcomer and connected him to people and opportunities in his new school that were parallel to the major interest of his heart.

I hope teachers like her know what a blessing they are!

—*Myra J. Martin*

Part Seven
SHAPING POTENTIAL

Our purpose extends far beyond teaching English, math, science, and social studies. We are shaping the minds of the young people who are the future of our nation. By planting seeds in these young minds and watering and fertilizing them, we can help them reach their full potential. One of the greatest rewards of teaching is watching these young minds blossom and grow. God's reward is presenting us with a bountiful bouquet.

A word spoken at the right time is
like golden apples on a silver tray.
A wise correction to a receptive ear is
like a gold ring or an ornament of gold.

—PROVERBS 25:11–12

The Little
BROWN BUNNY

Michelle was born deaf—totally deaf in one ear and profoundly deaf in the other. Her parents discovered this when she was only one year old. They taught her American Sign Language and lip-reading and fitted her with a hearing aid that provided the maximum amplification. Through preschool and kindergarten, she attended private schools with small classes where the teachers were very attentive to her limitations.

Then Michelle's family moved to a new community, and for the first time Michelle attended the local public school. This transition impacted her more than any other schooling experience. In the larger classroom, she realized the inadequacies of her English skills. Almost every day she came home from school crying, "I don't want to go to school!" Her mother hugged her, prayed with her about the situation, and continued to work on her language and speech skills so Michelle could overcome this difficult change.

For a hearing-impaired person, one of the most difficult obstacles to overcome is figuring out who is speaking in a large group. Although Michelle was great at reading lips, she became frustrated in a large classroom. By the time she could figure out who was talking, that person would have finished his or her comment or question.

Michelle's third-grade teacher, Mrs. Strom, could see that Michelle was struggling with this problem. But this delightful, grandmotherly woman with gray, wispy hair and a warm, friendly smile showed sensitivity to Michelle's needs by purchasing a little brown bunny that provided the needed solution. She told the class, "Children, in order to have permission to speak, you must be holding the brown bunny. So if you have something to say, raise your hand, and I'll hand you the bunny."

No one but Michelle and Mrs. Strom realized that the bunny was actually for Michelle's benefit. Now Michelle would always know who was speaking and would be able to concentrate on lip-reading. The rest of the class thought Mrs. Strom had just devised a fun game to keep them all from talking at once. And although the bunny accomplished this, too, the main purpose was for Michelle to be able to keep up with the flow of conversation in class.

This third-grade class with Mrs. Strom gave Michelle the confidence she needed to be mainstreamed into the public school system. And Michelle's parents and a speech therapist also worked with her constantly to hone her English skills. As she became more adept at reading lips, she relied less and less on sign language. But today she feels that learning sign language during her formative years was the step that placed her ahead of her classmates.

In high school she was a cheerleader, a model, and an excellent student. For the difficult subjects she had an interpreter, but for the rest of her classes she depended on lip-reading. Now she attends college and works part-time. Her speech is exceptional, although she does pronounce some words in a slightly irregular manner due to her profound hearing loss. This causes some people to ask her, "Where are you from?" They think she has a cute accent!

But her future might have been much less bright if not for a caring, gray-haired teacher—and a little brown bunny.

—*Susan Titus Osborn*

Not what we give, but what we share,
for the gift without the giver is bare.

—J. R. COWELL

She Was a
CHEERLEADER

Her brilliant blue eyes held me captive, her smile warmed my heart, and I decided Mrs. Kingston was beautiful. She gave me a hug and said, "Welcome to sixth grade, Judy. I'm glad you're here." The sick feeling in the bottom of my stomach began to fade a little as she directed me to my desk.

That was my first day at Crown Point Elementary School. My family had moved to California from Ohio just two months before. I still didn't know anyone and had been dreading this day all summer. It wouldn't have taken much for me to break into tears and run back to the safety of my home. I needed encouragement in the worst way.

Mrs. Kingston didn't look at my hand-me-down dress and worn shoes, or notice that I was taller than the other girls and overweight. She made me feel special from the very first day— and not just me. She treated the whole class the same way. She was everyone's favorite teacher. The class felt like a family—all for one and one for all. There were thirty-five of us! How did she do it?

We sang a lot in Mrs. Kingston's class. Every morning after we recited the Pledge of Allegiance, we would sing a rousing patriotic song. One time she stood by me as we sang "God Bless America." She turned to me and said, "Why, Judy, your voice is lovely."

I felt like a million bucks. Now that's the way to start a day!

With her encouragement, two of my friends and I worked on a song in Spanish with three-part harmony. Mrs. Kingston heard us practicing and asked, "Would you sing your song for the class during our unit on Mexico?" We even landed in a talent show on a local television program, where we won third place. When we returned to school, we were treated like celebrities—with a beaming Mrs. Kingston as our biggest fan.

Each morning I left my home not feeling good about the few clothes I had to wear, the idea that my mom and dad were divorced, and the fact that my mom had become an alcoholic to try and make it through the day. But when I entered that bright classroom with Mrs. Kingston at the helm pointing me in the right direction, I felt safe.

Praise was on her lips long before we realized this is what kids need most. In her class we'd often hear words like, "Your hand-writing is really improving," or "You made that story come alive with the expression in your voice," or "What a great idea that was." Her goal was to encourage, motivate, and shape the potential of her students. To this day I love to read "with expression," and I hear myself echoing her same words as I interact with my children at home or my students at school.

Sixth grade happened almost fifty years ago, but it seems like yesterday. Today I realize in my classes that there are often girls or boys who need a hug and a look from me that says, "I like you, and I care about you." I put my arm on their shoulders, look into their eyes, and give 'em a smile.

I hope they'll never forget me. I know I'll never forget Mrs. Kingston.

—Judith Scharfenberg

Encouragement is like premium gasoline.
It helps take the knock out of living.

—F. C. McKENZIE

Love and an
OLD TYPEWRITER

"I don't want to go to school," my seven-year-old son whimpered. I smiled and tried one more time to get the cowlick on the back of his head to lie down.

"Robbie, you're going to like your new teacher, make new friends, and have fun in second grade."

He looked down at his feet and pouted.

Linda came rushing out of her room. "Look, Mommy, I have my new dress on." My five-year-old daughter eagerly waited to start school. Life for my children seemed so different. Linda loved school and learned quickly.

Robbie had been diagnosed with communication and learning disabilities. Before he started school, we had enrolled him in speech therapy at the Long Beach University Speech and Hearing Clinic. He'd improved tremendously until he started kindergarten. Then he regressed. Multiple problems developed. Coordination problems, impulsiveness, and a short attention span made him disruptive in class.

He'd had to repeat kindergarten, and in the first grade other kids started to label him as dumb. Every day when he'd come home, I'd see a hurt in his eyes too deep for crying.

In the second grade, though, he'd be in a smaller classroom with other special-needs kids. He'd receive the individual attention he needed. As we climbed into the car, Robbie slouched down in his seat, and I hoped and prayed that special education would be the answer.

Mrs. Hanson greeted us when we entered Robbie's classroom. The atmosphere communicated a sense of well-being. Brightly colored posters hung on the walls. The science corner displayed a poster of the human skeleton. Paint easels stood in another corner, next to a color chart on the wall. There wasn't a spot that didn't have something of interest visible.

Robbie went over to a table where an old typewriter sat. Mrs. Hanson walked over to him and said, "Robbie, would you like to type your name?"

He grinned and nodded his head. His eyes danced with excitement.

I glanced around the room. Every child seemed occupied with some project. I slipped out of the room as Mrs. Hanson sat down at the typewriter with Robbie.

A month later, Mrs. Hanson held a special conference for parents. We each sat at our child's desk. I looked through Robbie's folders: an art folder, math folder, and spelling folder—all created within the first month.

Mrs. Hanson smiled and said, "In my class children learn.

Long before I began teaching special education, I had to develop a program to help my own son—a special-needs child. Each item in this classroom has a function—like the old typewriter. Using it, the children learn the alphabet and improve hand-eye coordination at the same time. Plus, they love typing. Remember that children with learning disabilities are not dumb. They just learn differently."

Mrs. Hanson not only helped these children, but also taught her students' parents. She helped us see the potential that each of our children had.

From that first day of school, Robbie never again said, "I don't want to go to school." Instead he eagerly looked forward to going. He discovered that he loved to paint and to build things. He learned about tools and their proper use. He gained an understanding about the human body. He kept a notebook of short stories he had written in class. More importantly, he gained confidence, his speech patterns improved, and his language comprehension increased.

As a professional teacher, Mrs. Hanson helped her students academically, but she also added a special ingredient called love. She helped develop character and insight that ultimately shaped their individual potential. Robbie developed skills in her class that he never lost.

—*Karen Kosman*

Love is a great beautifier.

—LOUISA MAY ALCOTT

Part Eight
CHALLENGING MINDS

In this fast-paced world of microwaveable food, computer games, and video arcades, it is hard to gain the attention of our young people. Yet we have an advantage as teachers by having their bodies present in our classrooms for a fixed amount of time each day. By making the lessons interesting and exciting, we can challenge their young minds to want to read and discover more about the world around them. We can teach them to think independently and reason for themselves. Life is full of challenges, and we can help children face those challenges with confidence.

I will instruct you and show you the way to go, with my eye on you, I will give counsel.

—PSALM 32:8

Do You
REMEMBER ME?

Great things are accomplished by talented people who believe they will accomplish them.

—WARREN G. BENNIS

One evening I was sitting in my office at the Christian college where I was an adjunct professor. Suddenly there was a knock on the open door. I looked up to see a young man who was about twenty years old with big brown eyes and curly black hair, smiling at me.

He said, "Hi, Professor Osborn. Do you remember me?"

I felt like I'd been put on the spot. He looked vaguely familiar, but I knew he hadn't been one of my college students. I finally said, "Yes, you do look familiar."

He laughed and replied, "Well, I'm not surprised you don't remember me. After all, it's been six years."

Six years? He would only have been fourteen! I thought to myself. Then I remembered who he was. "Jason! You came to the writers' conference I ran at Biola. You were the youngest conferee there."

"You *do* remember me!" He sounded thrilled.

"Yes, of course," I replied. I thought back to the young teen who was so charming and outgoing that he stole everyone's heart at that conference so many years before. I remembered that he was also very interested in learning how to write for publication so he could share his thoughts and the gospel with others. I knew at the time that he would go far in life.

"What are you doing now?" I asked.

"I'm a junior here in broadcast journalism. I emcee the 6:00 show on the campus radio station. You'll have to listen to me sometime."

I sighed. "Oh, I'd love to, Jason, but I teach a three-hour course on Monday nights, and that's the only night I'm here on campus."

"I know," he said shyly. "I found you in the course directory."

"But my name has changed. I got married a couple of years ago." I knew I looked puzzled to him as I tried to sort it all out.

Jason laughed again as he came to my rescue. "Your name is listed as Susan Titus Osborn, and you're teaching Creative Writing, so I knew it was you. When the listing said you taught at 6:00, I figured I'd find you at about 5:00 in the communication office, preparing your stuff."

Now it was my turn to laugh. "How right you are."

He stopped smiling and looked at me with a serious expression. "I'm so glad I had a chance to talk to you again. I wanted you to know what an impact the writers' conference and your encouragement had on me and on my high school and college class decisions. I love writing, and I want to be a broadcast journalist so I can impact the maximum number of people. You challenged me to pursue that course six years ago, and now I have a chance to say 'thank you.'"

I swallowed the lump that was forming in my throat, blinked back tears, and stared at the poised, self-assured young man standing before me. "And thank you, Jason, for taking the time to locate me. It means so much."

Now it was his turn to have tears in his eyes. But he quickly recovered and said, "Well, I'd better get ready to go on the air. Bye, Professor Osborn. See ya around.

"And again, thanks for everything."

—*Susan Titus Osborn*

English
POUNDS

"That'll be one English pound."

Reluctantly I handed over the piece of paper with the symbol of one pound sterling on it. I had misidentified the word *and* as a pronoun instead of a conjunction, and it was going to cost me.

You see, when we fourth graders at Thompson Elementary School walked into Mrs. Carmean's class, we knew she took the word *English* seriously. Her room was decorated with maps from England. She even wore the symbol for pound sterling on a chain around her neck.

"In this classroom," she said that first day of school, "we speak the King's English." She drew out the word *king* and ended it with a trill and hand flourish that conveyed royalty. "To help you remember to use the King's English, we have English pounds."

She began passing out small slips of paper to each row. The English pounds of Mrs. Carmean's class were hand-drawn and run off on a ditto machine. But I was soon to discover they had great value.

"When you answer a question correctly, you can earn one or more English pounds. If you use incorrect grammar, you will be fined one or more pounds. And at the end of the year, there will be a prize for the student with the most English pounds."

I fingered my starting allotment and became determined to win the prize by having the most pounds.

The English pounds took on lives of their own. We competed fiercely to earn them. Our hands shot up at each question.

We even began monitoring each other's speech on the playground. Hardly a recess went by without someone reporting that Lori had used *ain't* or Keith had said *brung*.

At the end of the year, I was tied with Dinah Pfefferly for the most English pounds. For extra credit Mrs. Carmean gave us a passage to read, in which we'd have to identify all the parts of speech. My hand shot up and she picked me.

I looked at the paragraph. *Okay, this is easy.* I began reading: article, noun, verb, adverb, participle, pronoun. *What? Oh, no.* There was a word I didn't know the part of speech for. I glanced up at Mrs. Carmean, but she was still looking at her copy of the paper. I tumbled the word over in my mind. I looked up again. "Uh, adjective?"

Mrs. Carmean nodded, not looking at me.

I quickly finished the passage and heaved a sigh of relief when she handed me seven pounds. I grinned, knowing now I was ahead of Dinah.

The next day, though, Dinah came into class and raised her hand first thing. "Mrs. Carmean?"

"Yes, Dinah."

"Last night I asked my dad about the passage we read yesterday. There was a word that Jennifer said was an adjective but it's not. We looked it up."

My heart started pounding, and I felt my face heat up.

Mrs. Carmean looked over the passage again. After a long moment she said, "Dinah's right. Jennifer, give back three of the pounds."

My eyes swam with hot tears as I blindly handed back the pounds. We were tied again, and I knew I wouldn't win.

Dinah and I remained tied through that week, and Mrs. Carmean gave both of us a prize. I don't remember what I won, but I gained the larger, lifelong prize of expunging *ain't* from my vocabulary, knowing how to speak the King's English, and having a great love of all things English.

When I traveled to England while in college, I thought of Mrs. Carmean when a street vendor said in a perfect cockney accent, "That'll be one pound, please."

—*Jennifer Tiszai*

English grammar is so complex and confusing for the one very simple reason that its rules and terminology are based on Latin—a language with which it has precious little in common.

—BILL BRYSON

Just Give It
THREE DAYS

To my delight and surprise, Lucille Godwin, my English professor at Mars Hill College, took time for many private talks throughout my years there, expressing interest not only in my academics but also in my relationships and in my future. Her calm, ladylike demeanor and poise impressed me whether I was listening to her lectures, conversing in her office, or visiting in her home.

Along with her husband, Dr. Joseph Godwin, she embarked on a four-year-long confidence-building campaign for my benefit. Both challenged me to see myself through God's mind, not just through my own distorted perceptions or those of others. In fact, Dr. Godwin's reassurance that I was "worth my weight in gold" still brings comfort when the scales and my clothes indicate a heaviness I find harrowing. Mrs. Godwin, however, is the one who deserves the credit for the most valuable advice I have ever received.

One day after the demise of a distressing romantic relationship, Mrs. Godwin invited me into her office for a heart-to-heart talk. Sensing that something was amiss because of my unusual listlessness during class, she asked, "What is bothering you, Dalene?"

I slumped into a seat across from her and poured out my tale of woe.

With a rueful smile, Mrs. Godwin admitted, "My prayers have been answered. I did not think very highly of the young man you were dating!"

Then she offered the following words of wisdom. "Dalene, you probably think what you're feeling couldn't be worse, but let me help you put it in perspective," she said, her bright blue eyes boring into my tear-streaked ones. "When Jesus was crucified, the disciples went through the darkest period in history. They thought their lives were at an end. Never had the world looked more hopeless. Never had their dreams been so shattered. Yet only three days later, look how the picture changed. Jesus rose from the grave, and with His resurrection He restored their purpose and their power."

Continuing, she challenged me to make a personal application. "When you are facing difficult times and must make hard decisions or deal with unbearable people or situations, just give it three days. Often things will look entirely different. Your focus will be much clearer and your hope restored. By then you will likely know what to do next. Just wait, trust, and pray. Then obey."

I lifted my head, took a deep breath, and gave her a wobbly smile.

"Thank you," I whispered, nodding. "I'll think about what you've said."

Not only did the "just give it three days" principle propel me through that trying situation, it has helped me through countless trials and challenges since. In addition I have passed it on to many others caught in discouraging or seemingly impossible circumstances.

Now when my heart and mind are challenged or over-whelmed, instead of giving in to despair, I just give it three days. I wait, trust, and pray. Then obey.

Thank you, Mrs. Godwin, for your impact on my life.

—*Dalene Vickery Parker*

The memory of you will bloom like a flower in the garden of my heart.

—CHINESE PROVERB

Part Nine
NURTURING HEARTS

Each child is born special to God, no matter how he or she looks or what physical or mental limitations are there. We need to keep this in mind whenever a child tries our patience to its limit. Chances are he is apprehensive, has low self-esteem, and is only looking for acceptance. By loving him and nurturing his heart, we can help him develop self-esteem. When we show our students how special they are, we allow God to show His love for them through us. We become His instrument for this worthy cause.

"I assure you," He said, "unless you are converted and become like children, you will never enter the kingdom of heaven. Therefore whoever humbles himself like this child—this one is the greatest in the kingdom of heaven. And whoever welcomes one child like this in My name welcomes Me." —MATTHEW 18:3-5

Here the heart may give a useful lesson to the head. —WILIAM COWPER

Lessons
WITH LESLIE

I'll never forget crying in the rest room with one of my students. The situation occurred one September on the first day of school when I was a veteran sixth-grade teacher. Earlier that morning I had started math class with the standard drills, quizzing the students on addition, subtraction, multiplication, and division facts. I used flash cards, mental math, and board problems to determine how much review was needed before the students would be ready for more complicated work. My drills were fast-paced, and my students responded well—all except Leslie.

She sat quietly with her hands folded in her lap, eyes focused on her desk. Before I could finish the drills, she burst into tears and ran from the room. As soon as possible, I gave seat work to the rest of the class, and I went out to find her.

My first stop was the girls' rest room, and there she stood, wiping her face with a paper towel.

"Leslie!" I folded my arms in front of me. I was prepared to scold her for leaving the classroom without permission, to lecture her on the importance of math drills. But something in her hurtful expression made me stop short. I waited for her to speak.

Within seconds, her words cascaded out like water from a fountain. Her parents had recently divorced. She and her mother had just moved into the area.

"Oh, Mrs. Danner," she sobbed, "I'm so afraid you'll call on me for an answer, and I won't remember to say the right thing as quick as you want. I was never in a class like yours before. I don't know how to think that fast. The numbers . . . they're just

. . . I can't . . . " Her voice trailed off as if the effort of the speech had drained her.

In that moment I saw myself at her age. I, too, had moved to a new school as a sixth grader. Although I was a good student academically, this unfamiliar situation flustered me. I was scared, unsure of myself, and unable to come up with fast answers. I had stomachaches and headaches, and I felt afraid in a classroom full of strangers. Hesitant to reply to even the simplest question from the teacher, I had remained silent.

Now I looked at Leslie and could see the same kind of troubled heart—like my own some years earlier—beneath her petite, vulnerable form. I knew she needed more from me than multiplication drills. I hugged her and shed tears with her. I told her, "You can stay in the rest room until you're ready to come back to class. I won't call on you during the first week unless you raise your hand."

Leslie and I became friends that day, though we never mentioned the tearful incident again. She went on to become an honor student in my class and soon enjoyed participating in math drills and other class activities. She also studied piano with me after school and advanced rapidly, performing in a recital at the end of the year.

During her time as a sixth grader, Leslie learned countless math and music lessons from me. More importantly, though, we learned from each other.

—Ruth McHaney Danner

Mrs. Rudsit
CARED

I was scared but excited as I entered the dormitory. It was my first extended time away from home. At eighteen I didn't have a lot of self-confidence or life experience. And I knew I would need both to accomplish my goal of becoming a registered nurse.

The struggle was fierce because of all the adjustments to other people and the extremely heavy scholastic demands. Many in my class didn't make it past the first semester.

It was not until after the trauma of losing so many in our class that I met Mrs. Rudsit. My first impression was of a wide smile and peals of laughter. She was the obstetrics instructor for our nursing class.

Her eyes sparkled with life, and her trim figure and dark hair made her look youthful although she was old enough to be my mother. I don't know how we got to be such good friends, but I do know why. Mrs. Rudsit cared about silly teenagers. Her bubbly personality showed in her active interest in my life.

This patient lady listened when I shared important things with her. She didn't make fun of me or deride me, which was probably hard sometimes. I think she is the first adult I ever knew who listened with such attention to the things of my heart.

During the stress of nursing school, I went through a depression and had an eating disorder. I was extremely thin and had to have special snacks to build up my stamina. I struggled with the sometimes horrifying situations involved in nursing.

But her concern for me remained constant. I knew I could talk to her about anything. It was the first time I really felt important. She may not feel she did much, but to that confused teen she gave a gift of enormous value.

Through her steady acceptance I started feeling like I was someone worthy. Her nonjudgmental attitude helped me make decisions that were right for me. Mrs. Rudsit's humor and laughter at my silly antics helped me laugh at myself. She had a contagious laugh that rang out at some of my crazy jokes.

She listened, laughed, and cried with me. She cared enough to tell me the truth. When I doubted my vocation as a nurse, she encouraged me to hang in there. She even helped me go on with my life when I wasn't sure it was worth it.

Mrs. Rudsit never gave the impression I was silly and unimportant. She always had time for me. And although I went through some serious problems during those years, she remained an anchor of strength and wisdom. Many years later, when my husband was without work, she provided a home for us. For over thirty-five years, she has been a good friend and mentor. When I look back, I think of her as the most important person in my life during that crucial time. She will always occupy a special place in my heart.

Mrs. Rudsit believed in me and helped me believe in myself. I will never be able to thank God enough for putting her in my life.

—Crystal J. Ortmann

We think of the effective teachers we have had over the years with a sense of recognition, but those who have touched our humanity we remember with a deep sense of gratitude.

—ANONYMOUS STUDENT

99

Harry

Harry was one of those kids you'd call "special." He was bigger than all the other fourth graders because, if he hadn't repeated kindergarten and second grade, he'd have been in the sixth grade. But Harry didn't care—at least he didn't seem to anyway.

Harry was slow at just about everything he did—slow at answering questions, slow at thinking, always the last one to get his work done. Most of the time he didn't even finish his work, so he often had to spend his free time trying to catch up. Yet although Harry never seemed to quite get there, he just kept on trying.

Harry moved so slowly, in fact, that when he walked down the halls many of his classmates would complain whenever they got stuck behind him in line. They started to tease him, and Harry quickly acquired the nickname "Turtle." But his teacher, Mrs. Robins, wasn't about to let that continue. So she made a plan. She decided to give Harry a special job. Mrs. Robins made Harry the "Official Caboose."

Whenever it was time for the class to line up and leave the room, Harry was to be the last in line. His job was to turn off the lights, then take one last look to make sure no one was left behind. Harry was faithful at his new job. It wasn't long before he started to walk proudly down the halls, even though he always trailed several steps behind his classmates.

The other kids in the class knew, however, that Mrs. Robins had given the "Official Caboose" job to Harry to help keep peace. Otherwise, anyone behind Harry would always be yelling, "Come on, Harry, hurry up! Why do you have to be so slow?"

Thankfully, Mrs. Robins was a smart teacher. She knew how to make Harry feel proud, not ashamed. She knew how to keep the other kids from picking on Harry.

One snowy day—the last one before Christmas vacation was to begin—Mrs. Robins gave her class their last assignment for the term. The instructions were to draw a picture of a gift that each student hoped to receive on Christmas morning. Then when the drawings were complete, the students were to gather on the classroom rug.

So with their colored pencils, crayons, and markers, the students carefully drew detailed pictures of the presents they longed for most. Harry sat thinking for a while as he watched the snowflakes fall outside the classroom window. When he finished deciding upon a gift he longed for, he took his pencil and drew a very big circle with two straight lines beside it. It was certainly nothing fancy, and there wasn't any detail to speak of, but it was all that Harry needed. And it was the best that Harry could do.

When the drawings were finished, the students gathered on the rug in front of Mrs. Robins. Then one at a time she held up each student's drawing for the whole class to see. "Tell us about your drawing," she said to each student, "and explain why this would be your favorite gift to receive on Christmas morning."

As Mrs. Robins held up the drawings, it was easy to tell what the pictures were. Most of the students had drawn presents such as new bicycles, sleds, puppies, skateboards, or the latest electronic toy.

But when Mrs. Robins looked at Harry's picture, it wasn't quite so easy. "Harry," she said, "tell us about your drawing. And tell us why it's a gift you'd like to receive."

Harry looked at Mrs. Robins as she held up his drawing of a very big circle and two straight lines. "It's a drum and drumsticks," he said proudly. "I need that gift so I can play Pa-rum-pa-pa-pum for baby Jesus!"

The room was silent. No one laughed at Harry.

—*Wendy Dunham*

Success in life is a matter not so much of talent as of concentration and perseverance.

—C.W. WENDTE

Part Ten
INSPIRING DREAMS

The words we speak today may inspire dreams that will last a lifetime in our students. Never underestimate the influence of a spark we can ignite that will set fire to those dreams waiting to burst into flame. Someday we will retire and leave the teaching profession, but we will leave behind a legacy in the hearts and lives we touched along the way. Twenty years from now a student may return to our hometown to look us up and say, "I'm where I am today because you taught me to dream. Thank you for giving me the confidence not only to dream but to follow my dreams. Now I hope to inspire my friends, coworkers, and family to follow their dreams."

He told them. "For I assure you:
If you have faith the size of a mustard
seed, you will tell this mountain, 'Move
from here to there' and it will move.
Nothing will be impossible for you."

—MATTHEW 17:20

Student
AT RISK

Student at risk. I repeated those words to myself as my husband and I walked into the vice principal's office. How was it possible that our fifteen-year-old son wore this dreaded label? We took seats at a large rectangular conference table where all of our son's high school teachers and the vice principal were already seated.

"Good morning," I said, glancing around the table apologetically. "Jim didn't want to ride with us. He took the bus but promised to be here on time."

The hands on the round clock on the wall pointed to 7:00 A.M. *Will he even show up?* I wondered. The meeting had been called to discuss his failing grades.

"Don't worry," Mrs. Baughn, the vice principal, said as if reading my mind. "If he doesn't come, it's okay."

Okay? I thought. *It's certainly not okay with me!*

At 7:05, a nervous adolescent boy wearing a baseball cap turned backwards and a scared look walked through the door, chewing gum. Our eyes met as he slipped into a seat between Mrs. Baughn and his P.E. teacher, Mr. Schmidt, at the far end of the table.

He sat a safe distance from Mom and Dad and close enough to the door to bolt as soon as the meeting ended.

Mrs. Baughn, a tiny woman who looked and spoke more like a loving grandmother than a high school vice principal, turned and said, "Jim, I think you know why I called this meeting today. Your parents, your teachers, and I are concerned about your grades."

Jim's eyes stared down at the table.

"I've asked all your teachers and your parents to be here this morning," she continued, "to see if we can help you improve your grades."

The room fell silent as Mrs. Baughn turned to Jim's math teacher.

"Jim doesn't fit the profile of a failing student," the teacher began. "He's quiet and cooperative in class and doesn't cause any problems. But he doesn't do the work."

Each teacher repeated the same story.

Mr. Schmidt, the P.E. teacher, was the last to speak. Looking squarely into Jim's anxious, deep blue eyes, he began, "Jim, I've been teaching for over twenty years, and I have never had another student with your kindness and sensitivity for others. When we play football, you are the only boy who throws the football to the girls.

"You are a very talented football player, but talent isn't everything. Without studying and achieving good grades, you won't be able to play football. I don't know why you are failing your other classes. You are an outstanding student who is making an

'A' in my class. I'd like to see you make the same effort in all your classes that you make in P.E."

For five minutes, Mr. Schmidt bathed our son with words of affirmation, instruction, and praise. Tears filled the eyes of every adult in the room, including Mrs. Baughn, who unashamedly wiped her eyes.

"Mr. Schmidt," Mrs. Baughn asked, as the first-period bell rang, "would you be willing to be Jim's mentor? Could he be your classroom aide and come to you with his problems?"

"Absolutely," he answered without hesitation.

That evening while my son and I practiced his driving in our neighborhood, he said, "Mom, will you tell me again what Mr. Schmidt said?"

"He said, 'I've been teaching for over twenty years, and I've never had another student with your kindness and sensitivity....'"

In that moment, I realized Mr. Schmidt's words had made a deep impact on our son's heart. With prayer and the caring guidance of Mrs. Baughn and Mr. Schmidt, I knew our son was no longer a student at risk.

—*Jeanne Getz Pallos*

The finest gift you can give anyone is encouragement.

—SYDNEY MADWED

Miss Ritter's
BIBLE

___

She almost always wore a simple black dress, but the black only made her gentle, smiling face shine more brightly. A splash of white trimmed her hemline, for—almost always—her slip showed. But what I remember most about my first-grade teacher is that her big, black Bible was always at her side.

The year was 1951, and I was a pupil in Miss Ritter's lively class at Roosevelt Public School in Norristown, Pennsylvania. Every morning just before the beginning of lessons, Miss Ritter summoned us to stand reverently by our desks as she took her big, black Bible and opened it to the twenty-third Psalm.

"Boys and girls, please rise."

Immediately we slid out of our seats and stood straight as soldiers. Not a student spoke or squirmed as our teacher slowly read the comforting words, for we instinctively knew that we had entered the presence of God.

Miss Ritter's melodious voice rang throughout the room. "The Lord is my Shepherd; I shall not want." The words instantly calmed my spirit. Although I didn't fully comprehend their meaning, I felt their healing balm wash over my troubled heart like warm oil.

Despite my tender years I had known much want: want of unconditional love, want of peace, and even want of food on occasion. Living in a home with serious problems, I had become an anxious, wounded lamb, untrusting and afraid. I did not know the care of a loving Shepherd; I knew only fear and emotional pain.

Day after day as Miss Ritter faithfully read the twenty-third Psalm, a dream began to take root within me. *Would this wonderful Shepherd that my teacher reads about every day ever want to become my Shepherd?* I wondered. How I longed for someone who would take care of me, who would never abandon me, and whom I could trust with all my heart!

To some of my classmates, Miss Ritter's big, black Bible did not attract particular attention. But to me it became the *focus* of my attention, perhaps because we did not have a Bible in my home. In fact, I do not recall ever having seen a Bible until Miss Ritter introduced the class to hers.

The way my beloved teacher treasured this Book drew me to it. She treated her big, black Bible with the highest respect and demonstrated great love for what it held within its pages. Little did I realize then that her example would birth in me an abiding love for this Holy Book and a deep hunger for what it contains.

As I look back, I recognize in Miss Ritter's daily reading of the twenty-third Psalm the marvelous love of God for a hurting little girl. In giving me this godly teacher, He provided me with a link to His love—a love I desperately needed.

Now more than fifty years later, the words of that beloved psalm still ring in my ears. I remember little else about first grade, but I shall never forget Miss Ritter. More importantly, I shall never forget her big, black Bible. Watered by her prayers, the seed of the Word of God she planted within me during that impressionable year has taken root and—by God's grace—has produced much fruit. The dream she inspired in me has come true. The Shepherd of Psalm 23 is now, indeed, my Shepherd!

—*Mary Ann Diorio*

The mediocre teacher tells.

The good teacher explains.

The superior teacher demonstrates.

The great teacher inspires.

—WILLIAM WARD

The Worst Thing
A TEACHER CAN DO

As was our custom while I checked the roll, my eleventh-grade students spent the first five minutes of class responding to the writing prompt I had placed on the board. This particular day's prompt began: "The worst thing a teacher can do is—" I couldn't wait to see how they filled in the blank.

Some students started scribbling furiously while others frowned in concentrated thought. After a few minutes I asked for volunteer responses. Nearly everyone had something to share.

At first the answers were routine and predictable. Demetria said, "The worst thing a teacher can do is give homework on weekends." Mildred chimed in with, "The worst thing a teacher can do is give a test on stuff you haven't studied." Keith added, "The worst thing a teacher can do is embarrass you in front of your friends."

Around the room we went, each student supplementing my collection of hints on how to teach and reach these young people better. Some of their suggestions I could accommodate; some were wishful thinking! The important thing was to let these teenagers know that I valued their input in the way we conducted our classroom.

Finally it was Ricky's turn. Tall and striking in appearance as well as mannerisms, when he stood, everyone turned to listen. He began only when he had my full attention. "The worst thing a teacher can do . . . " He paused, then repeated himself for emphasis. "The worst thing a teacher can do is *quit!*"

I inhaled deeply and raised my eyebrows in surprise. How could he possibly have known what I was thinking just that very morning?

At the end of my resources both physically and emotionally, I was seriously contemplating resigning mid-year. My sixty to eighty-hour workweeks had caught up with me, and I was running on empty. Essentially, my dreams for my family, my students, and myself had all been derailed by fatigue and frustration, and I was no longer willing to work so hard only to accomplish what seemed like so little.

Yet this young man had just capsized my plan in the space of one sentence. Ironically, he did not even belong in my class. Transferred to our school only a few days earlier, it was obvious Ricky did not require the remediation for which the class was intended. In fact, I had already recommended he be moved to a higher-level English class. He obviously had been sent my way, however, to deliver an important message. *The worst thing a teacher can do—is quit!*

"Thank you, Ricky. I needed to hear that," I responded, tears smarting at the corners of my eyes.

With those nine words, that young man inspired me to pick up the shattered pieces of my dreams and stay in the classroom. Because of him, I am still trying nearly twenty years later to motivate students to become competent, confident citizens, determined to do their best to live out their own dreams and make our country and world a better place.

May we never quit. And may we never quit dreaming.

—*Dalene Vickery Parker*

God stands as it were a handbreadth off, leaving his creatures room to grow in.

—ROBERT BROWNING

Contributors

Joan Rawlins Biggar, a former teacher, has written two series of adventure-mystery books for young people and has published a variety of articles, poetry, and short pieces. Between them, she and her husband, Hank Husby, have seven grown children.

Lanita Bradley Boyd is a freelance writer in Fort Thomas, Kentucky. Her writing springs from many years of teaching, church ministries, and family experiences. She believes that showing respect for each student is the key to good teacher-student relationships.

Stephanie Ray Brown is blessed to be Terry's wife, as well as Savannah and Cameron's mother. Whether it's teaching or writing, Stephanie enjoys sharing words. Stephanie's love of language is the result of her mother's instilling in her a love of books.

Joan Clayton is a retired teacher with thirty-one years in the classroom. She has over 450 published articles and is the author of seven books. Joan married her high school sweetheart fifty-four years ago, and they live in Portales, New Mexico. Her website is www.joanclayton.com.

Lonnie C. Crowe, a native of Wyoming, is retired after thirty years of teaching English. She currently is an area officer for Aglow International, a Bible teacher, a speaker for Christian groups, and a freelance writer.

Ruth McHaney Danner is a writer and quilter from Spokane, Washington. She has taught in public and private schools and now tutors in after-school programs. She wrote the inspirational book, *What I Learned from God While Quilting*, published by Barbour.

Dr. Mary Ann Diorio is a widely published author and professional speaker. She is founder and director of "Life Coaching for Professionals." Mary Ann and her husband are the parents of two grown daughters and reside in Millville, New Jersey.

Wendy Dunham is a wife, mom, inspirational writer, and registered therapist for differently-abled children. When she's not playing with her children, gardening, or doing laundry, she can be found at her computer, writing. Contact her at 3148 Lake Road, Brockport, New York 14420 or call 716-637-0535.

Bonnie Compton Hanson is author of the *Ponytail Girls* book series for girls plus other books, poems, stories, and articles (including stories in three *Chicken Soup* books). Contact her at 3330 South Lowell Street, Santa Ana, California 92707 or call 714-751-7824. Her email is bonnieh1@worldnet.att.net.

Karen Kosman is a wife, mother, grandma, CLASS graduate, and freelance writer. She is a contributing author in several bestsellers. Many diverse life experiences allow her to speak and write about healing for the hurting heart. Contact her at ComKosman@aol.com or call 714-670-8103.

Myra J. Martin is a pastor's wife. She and her husband, Mitch, have been married for twenty-two years and make their home in Nashville, Tennessee. Their son, Dustin, is seventeen and daughter Kristin is fifteen. Myra holds an associates degree in religious education. Myra's perspective is "Life is too transitory to ignore those encircling us."

Cia Chester McKoy is a full-time freelance writer and speaker who lives with her husband in Brookfield, Wisconsin. She is a CLASS graduate, and her speaking goal is to stir up spiritual hunger and hope in any women who have unconsciously trapped God's Spirit in a box. Contact her at ciamckoy@earthlink.net.

Janet Lynn Mitchell is a wife and mother of three. She is also an inspirational speaker and author of numerous articles and stories in compilations. Janet's latest book, *A Special Kind of Love*, coauthored by Susan Osborn, will be available in 2004. Janet can be reached at Janetlm@prodigy.net or by fax to 714-633-6309.

Susan Titus Osborn is director of the Christian Communicator Manuscript Critique Service. She is a contributing editor of *The Christian Communicator* magazine and an adjunct professor. She has authored twenty-five books. Susan and Dick have a blended family of five children and ten grandchildren. Contact Susan at Susanosb@aol.com.

Crystal J. Ortmann changed careers from nurse to freelance writer. Her writing covers many genres, from inspirational poetry and prose to fiction and nonfiction. It is her passion to inspire, encourage, and deepen the faith of her readers. She lives in Portland, Oregon.

Jeanne Getz Pallos is a former elementary teacher who is currently adjusting to an empty nest. She lives in Laguna Niguel, California, with her husband of twenty-nine years. She is a published author and leads a critique group in Southern California.

Dalene Vickery Parker is a teacher, writer, and speaker from Spartanburg, South Carolina. She has a heart grown rich with the influence of teachers and students in her life. Her husband, Pat, and children, Daniel and Susanne, are also great treasures.

Judith Scharfenberg is wife to Richard, mother of six, grandmother of eight, and a retired children's librarian, as well as an active author, speaker, and discipler. Her passion is encouraging everyone to put Jesus first in all they do. She says, "Being a wife and mom are the best jobs on earth."

Nanette Thorsen-Snipes has published over 450 articles, columns, and reprints in publications such as Focus on the Family's *LifeWise* and *The Lookout* and in more than fourteen compilation books. She is married to Jim and has four children and two grandchildren. E-mail her at nsnipes@mindspring.com.

Jennifer Tiszai is a wife and mother of two young children in Southern California. She writes devotionals, small group Bible studies, and website articles for one of the largest churches in the nation. She is currently working on her first novel.

LeAnn Weiss is founder and president of Encouragement Company. As the author of *Hugs for Friends* and the *Heartlifters* series, her paraphrased Scriptures are featured in over three million *Hugs* books as well as Lawson Falle's *Hugs and Heartlifters* greeting cards.